AF443906

THE
SOCIOLOGY
PRACTICUM

FINDING YOUR VOICE
IN THE WORKING WORLD

EUGENE JL LIM

Also known as Socio Empath

First ebook edition: December 2019

First print edition: January 2020

Cover image by Michael Frattaroli

Web: https://socioempath.com

IG: @socioempath

FB: Socio Empath

Goodreads: Eugene JL Lim

Contents

Recess: Weaving Webs of Interaction 63

Assess: Probing Pitfalls and Intersections 83

Finding Your Voice: To Speak and Be Heard 103

"We are Durkheim of people who can't get full Marx,
Weber we like it or not."

1

Putting Sociology into Practice

You can do anything you want!

With concealed delight, I held the leaflet to my face again. There it was, a four-coloured wheel spanning 8 clusters of occupations. There was research, there was policy, there was social service, there was communications. Phew, I thought. When I had told people I wanted to switch to the arts—having journeyed from neighbourhood math prodigy into the Science stream—people around me panicked. *What are you going to do, be a teacher?* Where I lived, in Singapore, teaching is a conventional choice. Not prestigious, but certainly respectable. Though I have immense respect for the occupation, I was pleased to find out it was not a Sociology graduate's only option.

It was freeing to not have to commit to a profession at the tender age of 19, unlike my peers signing up for programs in Law, Medicine, or Engineering. Lawyers and doctors were the highest-status professions and certainly ideal for many high achievers. But even if I had the grades, I did not have the heart to dissect someone else's arguments or body parts. It pains me. As for Engineering, I never once bothered. As someone who mused abstractly about topics of self and society, material disciplines appeared to me as nothing more than irrelevant detail.

Once I was convinced Sociology is the one for me—and likewise my sceptical parents—it was time to think about what I wanted in my future work. The first criteria was: Free time. I wanted a job from 9 to 5—or 9 to 6 these days—with no overtime. It was not due to laziness; no one who has clocked in 8 productive hours for the day should be made to feel guilty for leaving on time. What I needed was time to do what I like: To read, to write, to reflect on life, to keep relationships alive. These mattered most to me. As for the choice of occupation, I was happy to bide my time. I'd rather stay on the ground than scale the top of the wrong tree.

Several years have passed since. I graduated with a Bachelor's and entered the workforce. Guess what I did? I entered market research. It was a swift entry. In just my second week, I worked past 11pm. If only I had time to recover or to forget... but no. The next day, it was 4am. I laughed at the insanity of opening the house door to my parents having breakfast. Eventually I stopped laughing, because I remembered what it was that I wanted. I wanted time to do what I like. Yet as months passed, I realized I could never leave at 6. I could not possibly forfeit on deadlines and leave coworkers to die. If it meant staying up on a weekend or public holiday, so be it. Everyone did it.

There was no choice... right?

Sociology's 1st Gift: Releasing Illusion of Free Will

This is the first lesson Sociology teaches: Having no choice. There is a popular notion these days, promoted by self-help gurus and social media influencers, that we are free to do whatever we want. Yet this is only an illusion. Responsibilities exist. You can leave work undone. You can fight with your boss. You can quit your job. You can stay at home. You are technically free to do all these. But practically, you are not free from repercussions. Colleagues can alienate you. Bosses can demean you. Future employers can judge you. Family members can nag at you. They are also free to, aren't they?

If you care about securing a decent quality of life, you cannot act irresponsibly. YOLO ("you only live once") is an anthem for those who seek freedom, but it may as easily be adapted for use by their naysayers. Do you want to study now or do you want to be swept along by the ceaseless waves of school assessments into lower and lower-paying jobs? Do you want to work overtime or risk losing your job at the next downturn and plunging your family into not just debts but marital or existential tensions? Come on, YOLO!

Is this a false choice? No doubt. But those with the sociological imagination will recognize the underlying issue of agency versus structure. For non-Sociology students, this can simply be understood as a matter of freedom and constraint. If your actions and the actions of others affect what is possible later in your lives, then are you really free to do anything you want?

Most of what I learned in Sociology involves understanding all the different ways by which our freedom is restricted. We are restricted by not just the judgment of courts but the judgment of people. We are restricted by not just the families we are born into but the peer groups which take us in—or don't. We are restricted by the economy we live in because it determines the jobs we get to do and the people we get to work with. These are often not within our control. Even so, we are very skilled at interpreting all we do as acts of freedom.

As you learn to see the world from the outside view, and how your free will is influenced by so many external factors, your sense of self may be threatened. Nobody likes living in limbo. Unless there is a solution, a better way of perceiving reality that is empowering, you will easily revert to illusions just as a way to keep sane and function in the face of continual challenges at work and in life.

Sociology's 2nd Gift: Finding Paths to Freedom

This is a challenge Sociology can take on, even if it rarely does. Knowing where our shackles are can be frightening, but it also gives rise to the possibility of removing them. The problem is that there is no consensus in Sociology on how these shackles can be removed. The most radical involves revolution, or a fundamental overhaul of the economic system. This is the view of Karl Marx, and maybe Max Weber as well. However, if our individual freedom hinges on achieving what he envisions as the "ideal" state of social organization, then we might be doomed to a life of misery.

On the other hand, Émile Durkheim—the other founding father of Sociology—believes that individuals function best with moderate levels of social regulation. This means having rules to live by, whether enforced by law or agreed upon by most people. Having such shared norms keep all of us in check. Just as too much regulation can disempower people, too little regulation can land people in a state of perpetual unhappiness, always wanting more. As a society, complete freedom or anarchy gives rise to chaos. From this point of view, placing constraints on everyone helps in protecting the freedom of each one. Having systems in place which reflect shared norms is optimal for all of us.

Both contain an appetite for social engineering, where we try to alter social structures to resolve personal problems. This makes sense from the view of sociologists, because they are the experts in revealing the constraints society place on individuals and how deeply-rooted these constraints are. I agree that we should strive to refine systems to lessen their burdens on individuals. But I believe that freedom at its heart is an individual journey. We can increase the space for freedom by altering systems, but no system or revolution by itself can determine how well we use this space for freedom.

Freedom must ultimately be negotiated in how we interact with people, within existing systems of realities. This is where the likes of Charles Cooley and Erving Goffman can also enter the conversation. By examining how social interactions can affect our selves—our identities and decisions—we can learn to be more sensitive to the pockets of opportunity to create more freedom not only for ourselves, but also for the others we interact with.

If we let go of the mirage of absolute freedom, we can begin the work of increasing relative freedom. What Sociology does is to give us the conceptual basis to change locations, change systems, and change our ways of interaction. This is its second lesson: Making your own choices. We can become more free, whether we choose to stay put or move on.

Realities At Work

When I was still in school, I could hide behind idealistic notions of what Sociology could do. I was enamoured by the sociological imagination, the ability to see personal problems as public issues and vice versa. In our times of snap judgments, I believed this to be our most urgently needed quality of mind. Promoting the sociological imagination, in itself, will make the world better. This is in hindsight a hard sell, because pretty much everyone thinks that they are right, that the world would be better if everyone would just think like them. Who am I to say that thinking sociologically is our best antidote?

Having stepped into working life, I realized the greater concern became: Who cares? Even if I was right, that what our world needs is the sociological imagination, who would bother? Why would they bother? If I had to work late into the night regularly, I wouldn't want to spend my remaining hours agonizing over how flawed my perception of reality might be. I just want to sit on the couch and sleep. I just want to make life more tolerable by spending time on the things and people I like.

Yet this is far from optimal. Unless we are already doing what we love, with no major caveats attached, we can do better. What we most *urgently* need are not manuals on how to think—as important as that may be—but manuals on how to live. If we cannot find rhythms we are comfortable with when working, we will struggle to find the energy to do what we find meaningful, things we believe we ought to do. For me, it is to read, to write, to reflect on life, to keep relationships alive.

And so, I resigned. I left a culture which didn't allow me to breathe. I moved to one which allowed me to. I cannot say I became all set. Yet enough was different that I could finally start work on my first book, the book you are now reading. It is a practicum, a supervised practical application of previously studied theory. It is a synthesis of what I have learned in school and what I have experienced at work. It is a note to self and, hopefully, a gift to you.

The Sociology Practicum

This is a 6-week hands-on module designed for both Sociology and non-Sociology students. Anyone who is or expects to work as an employee to any organisation and wants a fulfilling life is encouraged to enrol.

This week, you have been introduced to Sociology and what it can offer for working men and women. Over the next three weeks, you will explore three ways you can exercise your voice in the working world: Express, Transgress, and Recess. Each of them creatively builds on ideas from the three major schools of thought in Sociology: Functionalism, Conflict Theory, and Symbolic Interactionism. You can find in each approach several lessons which you can apply to any occupation or workplace you are in or want to enter.

In the 5th week, we will discuss how you can move forward from the three approaches at your disposal. You will be walked through the potential pitfalls involved in each approach and given suggestions to address them by borrowing lessons from the other approaches. You will be encouraged to go deep rather than broad. In the final week, we will revisit what it means to find your voice in work and in life, and unravel what it takes to speak and be heard.

While Sociology thinkers and concepts are referenced throughout, they are included only to the extent that they can enrich your understanding of work. Your life is yours. What matters is that you take what you need to start making your life better. Whatever you believe, escape is not your only option. You may not be able to do anything you want. But you can find out what you want to be, and work from there.

2

Express: Picking Paths of Least Resistance

Do what you love!

This music to the ears of dreamers will no doubt be interrupted by mocking from the lips of pragmatists: *Doing what you love is the lie teachers tell you to protect your innocence. Doing what you love does not pay the bills. Once you reach working age, people start telling you the truth. Try loving what you do. If that doesn't work out, tough luck mate, welcome to the real world. You just have to live with it.*

When your favourite lullaby screeches into heavy metal, the instinctive reaction is to recoil. The working world is nothing like school. Knowledge gives way to profit, and hard work may not be acknowledged, let alone rewarded. You are expected to slave for the company, past midnight if necessary. Processes are clunky, the people you have to work with equally unwieldy. You cannot skip a workday like you skip a class. You cannot leave, because you have to work to live. This is a lot of constraint to live with.

Why not, you wonder... Why not find a comfy job which allows you to leave work on time, even if it is unfulfilling? Why not just become a freelancer or influencer and take charge of your own time? If the working world corrupts us and traps us in an endless grind, should we not protect ourselves by minimizing our time and investment in it? Why not escape? Why not be free?

I am a dreamer, so it's no surprise that I had entertained such thoughts for years. Rather than deciding on an occupation and working towards it, I felt I had to zoom out and think about the ideal life I eventually want to have. It then becomes a matter of deciding which compromises I am willing to make. Finding a job becomes a process of elimination, of crossing out the ones which contradict my life goals.

If I could just do what I love... I would read, I would write, I would reflect on life, I would keep plenty of relationships alive. I would pursue other creative endeavours and commit more time and energy to socially meaningful causes. I wanted freedom when it comes to my creative pursuits, so they have to be pursued outside of regular work, not part of it. It seemed obvious that my top priority should be to find a job that provides the least resistance to these pursuits.

When I finally started working, I realized this is not straightforward at all. Finding a job that demands little and lets you leave on time is not as good an option as it looks.

First, such a job usually pays too little or is difficult to find and keep. Second, such a job will not help you find your voice in this world. Instead, the chronic lack of stimulation can actually drain you and stick with you even after you leave the office. You lose more than you gain.

So what should you do?

Resistance as a Social Fact

Let's start again with doing what you love, since it is music to our ears. It is what you gravitate to instinctively when you have free time—if not now, then when you were a kid. It is what you may still do even when you have no free time. You may not know or remember what this is. But if you do know something which gives you joy, that you do freely, why would you resist also getting paid for doing it?

If you exist in a physical and social vacuum, with obligations to no one apart from yourself, then you may be free to act as you wish. Since the only resistance which exists is internal—psychological—doing what you want to do is both the path of least resistance and the path of most self-expression. But none of us live in isolation. We exist in spaces inhabited by other people. Our actions will bring about reactions from others. As reactions are not always affirmative, there will always be some form of external resistance. In this case, doing what you want to do the way you want may generate substantial amounts of external resistance, to the extent that it becomes neither a path of least resistance nor a path of most self-expression. It is easy to sprint on a running track, but try doing it in a peak-hour train.

Having external resistance—or social regulation—is not in itself bad though. What happens if we have too little social regulation? Émile Durkheim, often considered the founding father of modern Sociology, believes that this will result in anomie. Anomie is a condition where individuals are no longer restrained and instead allowed to unleash their infinite desires. This is far from an optimal state. When individuals believe they can do anything and get anything they want, they only set themselves on an endless cycle of disappointment. They will be stuck in a rut of perpetual unhappiness, always wanting more. In the worst case, suicide becomes the only option to satisfy the desire for complete freedom or liberation.

Since complete freedom is never attainable, we need to tame our infinite desires. For Durkheim, the individual is not capable of doing so. Individuals have to be constrained by a force external to them, namely society. This force can be applied through laws, or act more subtly through social norms. Society is thus not just a collection of individuals. Society imposes external resistance on individuals, bringing order to an otherwise chaotic world. More radically, seen through Durkheim's eyes, society also translates external resistance into internal resistance, which helps individuals to function more optimally.

This sets up a paradox. If resistance can help us, should we even be picking the paths of least resistance? Before we decide on this, we first need to learn to look at external resistance without leaping to judgment and rushing to escape.

Accepting External Resistance at Work

When you are new to the workforce, armed with a degree, it can be easy to have inflated expectations. You might expect a higher-than-average pay. You might expect to leave work on time every day. You might expect to work at a place near where you stay. You might expect to have flexible work arrangements, or at least flexi-hours. You might expect extensive medical and wellness coverage. You might expect a cool boss and chill colleagues. You might expect sponsored trainings and overseas trips. You might expect frequent pay revisions and promotions. You might expect to make full use of your talents.

A dream job will have everything you want. But, can you wait for it to come?

Even if we expect a lot, it is not fair to label us a strawberry generation, categorically unable to take any form of hardship. Many of us have grown up in a consumerist culture, where we are encouraged to not just customize our clothes and replace our phones, but also pick our modules and rate our teachers. We cannot blame only young people for the lifestyles businesses feed them—through advertising or technology—and for expecting the working world to share the same set of values.

Yet this does not mean that our consumerist culture is healthy. The more we inhabit the role of a consumer, the less energy we have to be a creator. Work is not leisure. We pay for one, we get paid for the other. Finding your voice requires you to put in hard work, to express your gifts, to essentially be a creator. These days, it is easy to leap to the conclusion that you need to escape paid employment as soon as you can. You would rather do freelance work, start an online business, or take a shot at becoming an influencer. It is good to take greater ownership of your work. But you cannot expect it to be easy!

If freedom of expression is what you seek, taking all salaried options off the table does not sound like the best way about it. Increasingly, we live in societies with large populations and a high degree of specialization and inter-dependence in corporate units. More and more jobs in the market require us not just to work in teams, but with stakeholders across departments and organizations. This is true not just in the corporate world, but in government, in education, in social services, in entertainment. The list goes on. If you detest any form of external resistance, you will effectively shut yourself out of all the jobs existing across these fields. You will also shut yourself from all the domain experts you can work with and learn from up close.

But if you can live with resistance, you keep your options open. And the eventual move to self-employment remains an option you can pursue sometime in the future.

Work as a Source of Belonging

So far, I have been treating work as something you are forced to live with. Think of it as having a distant cousin staying over at your place for the summer. This relative's presence disrupts your natural rhythms; you are forced by the noise to wake up early, you get more concerned about keeping things tidy, and you cannot go to the toilet as freely as you used to. You have no choice but to adapt your lifestyle accordingly, for as long as you need to. Just like your day job. But let's now consider the flip side: Might working in group environments bring benefits? Can this relative's presence actually be useful?

Let's hear again from Durkheim!

Over a century ago, Durkheim had the theory that societies are transforming in terms of social solidarity, or how people belong together. In earlier societies, people inhabit similar roles as the units of society tend to be alike. This produces mechanical solidarity, which is based on a strong moral culture, regulating the thoughts and actions of individuals. They mostly follow a standard set of norms. But as populations ballooned and structural units became more diverse, roles became more specialized and interdependent. As more and more of us start to do different things, it becomes more difficult to enforce a binding set of rules for everyone. Yet society does not simply disintegrate. People remain bonded in a different and more abstract way which stresses respect for the freedom of individuals. And this is called organic solidarity.

But clearly, such a form of bonding is far weaker. On one hand, it catapults the risk of anomie: Endless desire, disappointment, maybe suicide. On the other hand, social integration is weakened. When there is too little social integration, people develop an overly individualistic attitude. This is increasingly common as several forces have worked to lessen the integrative functions of family, religion, region and neighborhood. And what happens when people live too much in their own worlds with few people to confide in and share in their experiences? In the worst case, for someone who feels like their existence matters to no one, suicide.

Eventually, Durkheim found a structural solution to all of these problems: Occupational groups. Since occupational groups likely involve people who share similar interests and experiences, they can be a source of social integration. Having people like you working alongside you also helps to lessen the monotony of specialized jobs. So while you may hate going to work on a Monday morning, the five days at work should actually provide you the necessary social integration to protect you from psychological problems. The distant cousin may appear to be driving you insane, but could actually be helping to keep you sane.

If you follow Durkheim's line of thought, you should expect more from work than just a salary. You should feel like you are part of a larger collective. You should feel like you belong. Resistance—in terms of social regulation—can help you in taming your infinite desires, but it is not a goal you should seek. It is only a means to an end. Even as you learn to accept that you cannot have all you want at work, that there will always be resistance at work, you should learn to be more conscious of what you need in order to express yourself, and seek the paths of least resistance.

How can you figure out the paths of least resistance?

Finding Paths of Least Resistance

Just as institutions ought to serve functions for society, individuals can also take on suitable functions in society. It is at this point that we need to move beyond Durkheim. Durkheim's ideas are revolutionary for his time, and remain rather revelatory in our time. Yet in general, a functionalist approach focused on structures and collectives risks being overly prescriptive. We cannot count on it to help us discover our selves. For this purpose, I will borrow a tool developed in psychology: Holland's Theory of Career Personalities, which can also be referred to as RIASEC when used in profiling tests.

John Holland's theory emerged decades after Durkheim. Apart from matching individuals into one of 6 dominant types, Holland's theory also looks into classifying work environments into the same 6 dominant types. Work environments can be profiled not only by the profiles of the people working in them, but also by the types of work being done in them. This builds on the paradigm of person-environment fit, making it highly compatible with Sociology. It recognizes that our capacity to thrive in any work environment is not merely a matter of doing what we love or doing what we are skilled in, but also where we work in and who we work with.

Some of you may react instinctively: *How can you fit people into just 6 types?* But is that really the case here? While there are 6 dominant types, the types can be placed in a sequence from greatest to least preference. Instead of 6 types, there can theoretically be 6 x 5 x 4 x 3 x 2 x 1 = 720 types. Even if we reduce it to the first 3, as is often done in profiling tests, there are 6 x 5 x 4 = 120 types. This is already easily more than the number of types of people you can list from the top of your mind, or the number of people who you know well enough to give useful career advice to, without the use of a profiling tool like this.

This theory of vocational personality types comes with ample research. The RIASEC types (Realistic, Investigative, Artistic, Social, Enterprising, Conventional) are found to exist and be broadly applicable to different demographics and populations of individuals, though variations inevitably exist. While research into work environment types is more scant, it generally supports the theory. There is also strong evidence that person-environment fit, as measured by the RIASEC profiles, predicts stability and satisfaction in occupations, with jobhoppers often seeking new environments which are more congruent with their types.

The key lesson here is that it is important to work in an environment which supports your individual needs. You may be doing things you like, but in an organization which places a low value on your gifts. You may be proud of the quality of your work, but face constant resistance in a workplace with individuals whose types clash with yours. You may be in the right occupation, but the wrong organization. Resistance is specific to each person and each environment, so it is vital for you to look closely at both in order to assess the degree of fit. The RIASEC test appears to be a good basis for us to do so, since it is tailored for the purpose of helping individuals discover work which fits their inclinations, and is built on a theory well-regarded within the academic sphere.

~ ~

Practicum 1: Profiling Yourself

Take the time to do a RIASEC profiling test now. The RIASEC test involves a battery of 5-point scale questions asking whether you like or dislike specific tasks. What you should get in return are scores for all 6 vocational types, giving you an indication of the kinds of work which can energize you. Since you are trying to understand your vocational preferences, your skill levels should not be a consideration at all. Keep in mind to answer based on what you would like to do, not what (you think) you can do. Several free versions of the profiling test exist online, which can easily be found by typing '*RIASEC test*' or '*Holland Code test*' into search engines.

If there is ambiguity in the results—with some of the scores rather close—I recommend trying one or two different versions of the test on different days. This is because the tasks presented in each version can vary substantially, which means that the results you get may not necessarily reflect your actual types. Doing different versions can help you to confirm your type or make you think more deeply about what working style you truly prefer.

Doing them on different days helps you to mentally distance from the classification and lessen the likelihood that you give responses which will engineer the results that you want. You should never allow your self-image to obscure self-understanding.

I also recommend doing the same version of the test again from time to time, especially if you do not feel connected to your latest profile. There are two main reasons why this might be the case. First, you may not have discovered what you really like. You may not have been given the opportunity to do certain activities you like, or to do them in certain ways. Second, you may have lost touch with what you really like. You may have assumed an alternative identity under the weight of expectations from your family or community or school or workplace. While underlying vocational types should not easily change, new experiences and stages in life can make you more aware of what you really like. Redoing the test will help to ensure you are equipped to make the right career decisions at any point in time.

Practicum 2: Profiling Occupations

Doing the RIASEC test and understanding yourself is only half the work done. The other half concerns the environment you work in or want to work in. This is no straightforward task. After all, work is not just about what you do. Work is also about who you do it with, and how. You may not gain such information into any organization unless you join them. So let's step back first from work environments and look more generally at occupations.

Not all occupations are created equal. There are some occupations which you will struggle in no matter what you do, because they are not a good fit to your personality preferences. Picking a suitable occupation is thus of primary importance. The easy way is to type '*RIASEC occupations*' into search engines. Most websites will allow you to access a list of occupations along with their three-letter codes. Some will allow you to input your personal three-letter code and generate a list of compatible occupations. You can then click into these occupations and learn more about the typical work tasks and activities along with the skills and knowledge required.

If you have yet to formally enter the workforce, or are thinking of switching to a different profession, the O*Net Online portal is that nerd you can count on. Few can give you more insight into such a wide range of occupations in as efficient a manner. Apart from the skills and knowledge and credentials required, the portal also gives indications into work context, work styles and work values. Work context includes items like frequency of emails, contact with others, time pressure, importance of accuracy, freedom to make decisions. Work styles includes items like attention to detail, integrity, stress tolerance, innovation. Work values includes items like independence, recognition, relationships, support. You can also toggle the main tab, which will show you specific percentages for most of the categories, likely based on surveys on samples of people working in these occupations. These inform the RIASEC profiles for each occupation.

But there is a caveat. The occupational reports are built on data in the United States. If you reside or work outside the United States—I am Singaporean, for that matter—the credentials, work environments and job outlook can vary quite substantially. Even so, there is a lot you can learn about diverse occupations before going for any interviews or signing any contracts. I, for one, would have gained much from consulting this portal before I formally entered the workforce.

Beyond occupations, you may also want to profile work environments before joining them. This is tricky, but there are some ways to get more information. First, interact with people who work in that organization. Be mindful, though, that what people tell you may deviate greatly from the reality you eventually find yourself in. There are numerous reasons why this can happen, not least differing personality preferences. Second, observe your interviewers. These are likely the people you have to work closely with, and it will be good to make a preliminary assessment on whether your working styles are compatible. Again, be mindful that just like you, they may be projecting a different persona in the context of an interview. Third, ask the right questions during interviews. Find out how the organization is structured, where you will be situated in that structure, and what they expect from you. The more you ask, the more you can map out your potential workplace. Nonetheless, your interviewers may not tell you—or are not able to tell you—the full story. Ultimately, there is no substitute for signing on the line and judging for yourself.

Practicum 3: Profiling Work Environments

Let's say you have found an occupation which matches two or three letters of your RIASEC code. You found a job in that occupation and signed a contract. But after some time on the job, you find that it was not quite what you had expected. You are not enjoying yourself at work. This is not entirely surprising. You and your ex-coursemate can choose to work in the same economy, the same industry, the same position even, yet wind up with vastly different experiences. Before you tender your resignation, it may be worthwhile to first examine your work environment more closely.

It is possible that despite extensive research before joining the organization, you feel disconnected from the work you do. Even if O*NET or other portals have indicated a perfect or close match between you and your occupation, the organizational goals and structures may override what's typical for occupations. For instance, being a designer in a film company is going to be different from being a designer in a marketing agency. Being a clerk in an MNC is going to be different from being a clerk in a startup. Not all jobs in an occupation are created equal.

What can you do? First, retake the RIASEC test if you suspect your preferences have changed. You must however be cautious of confusing negative experiences at work with the work itself. Second, profile the types of work you are doing to see if they deviate from the occupational codes. Some occupations involve diverse work tasks, which organizations tend to divide across specialized teams. Even if you are a good fit for an occupation, your specific position may deviate significantly from what is typical of the occupation. Third, profile the types of work which exist in your organization. If an organization is dominated by occupational profiles which contradict yours, you may find it more difficult to function optimally. This is because the objectives of other job functions will likely be prioritized over yours. Assess whether the organizational structure allows you to thrive, and whether there are any actions you can and are willing to take to reduce the resistance you currently face.

It is also possible that you are actually pleased with the work you get to do, but still feel a sense of unhappiness at work. Instead of dismissing it as the syndrome of a strawberry generation, take the time to reflect on your emotions. Ask why you feel resistance. You most likely have tensions with other people at work. You may not even notice it, because the tensions only arise in certain situations.

What can you do? First, identify the people you have tensions with. They can be your bosses, immediate colleagues, direct clients, etc. Think about specific incidents at work which surfaced these tensions. Second, profile these people using the RIASEC model. When you have difficulties working with others, it is easy to just cast them as unreasonable. Sometimes the problems just stem from a lack of understanding due to differing interactional styles. Getting them to do the RIASEC test *and* share their results with you may not be achievable, especially if the tensions have already boiled over. If so, you have to resort to a more qualitative approach of mapping observed behaviours at work to the 6 types. Seeking a third opinion here may be wise. Third, find ways to reduce or resolve the tensions. If you cannot find the resources within to do so, look out for others with more compatible profiles who you can seek. They can either mediate the tensed relationship or provide an escape route which bypasses the need to deal with the source of your work frustrations.

Practicum 4: Growing Through Resistance at Work

Holland's RIASEC theory provides us with plenty of tools to work with, wherever we are in our career journeys. However, as you dive into close analyses of your vocational personality and your work environments, you must keep this in mind: There is no perfect job. There is no job in the world which can satisfy every desire you have.

Every occupation and job requires us to perform a diverse range of tasks—if not continually, then from time to time. There will always be tasks you like and tasks you dislike. You cannot say no to every task you dislike. This is the case even if—especially if—you are doing freelance work or running your own business. When you are at the helm, you gain materially from every task you accept. You have to satisfy the demands of your customers or risk ruining your reputation. In this sense, it may be easier when you are a salaried employee. Even so, there is surely a limit to the number of tasks you decline before you are sent packing, or given the collective treatment which makes you want to start packing.

Every occupation and job also involves you in social relationships. If you are an employee, you have to work alongside other employees. If you are a freelancer, you have to work with your clients. If you are a boss, you have to lead your employees. All of these people have their own work personalities and own expectations. You cannot reasonably expect to have your way every time. Your colleagues will alienate you, your clients will ditch you, your employees will leave you. To function at work, you must learn to accept resistance and be willing to compromise. Sometimes, it makes the products of your work better. Sometimes, it does not. But you can learn to adapt, to devise ways to make things work better.

When you do find jobs which really fit you, there is still the problem of access. You may not have the credentials or work experience to even qualify for the first interview. This is often the case when you are early in your career or looking to enter a different occupation. You have to meet rejection with patience and proactiveness. If you know what you are lacking, take the time to bridge the gap. You can enrol in courses which relate to the occupation of interest. You can develop relevant skills at your current job. The harder you have to work to land a job, the more you will cherish it.

Cultivating an acceptance for resistance is an inner journey. Durkheim believes that individuals cannot do it on their own; they need the regulation of society to keep them in check. I reckon that we can make use of such regulatory forces—not least from work—to move forward in our inner journey. Your body is the best place to start, because all resistance—internal and external—is felt by the body. The body is your richest source of data, available at any time—but to you only. No one else can do this for you.

The more you can listen to the heavy metal in your bones and muscles, without screaming or running away from it, the richer the possibilities which await you in the workforce. When you stop instinctively saying No to any form of resistance, when you learn to live with resistance, new paths of lower resistance will open up to you unexpectedly. It is when you can live with constraint that you actually gain more freedom, to narrow down and land the occupations which speak to you and allow you to speak, and express yourself in environments producing less resistance than you have learned to live with, in places where you can say you belong.

3

Transgress: Seizing Sites of Contestation

Change the world!

You may or may not recall the time when your world shifted. It could have been in your adolescence, or later. It could have evolved over a long while, from the bits and pieces placed into your palms from the passing remarks of your father, your mother, your overly-concerned relatives and your social media feeds. There could have been a single incident which shattered your rose-tinted image of the world. The world is not as beautiful as you thought. The world can be really selfish and cruel.

What happens after this revelation—along with the resultant shock or sadness or indignation—can vary a lot, depending on the stories you have been told or have seen for yourself. Some of you may feel a sense of resignation. If you have a father who kept his head down for three decades in a job he has no passion for just so he can pay the bills for your family, it will not be difficult to learn a thing or two about the virtue of accepting life in its ragged imperfections. When it is your turn to work, you may naturally gravitate to stability. If your boss tells you, *just do your job and you will be fine*, you will be quite pleased.

In contrast, the rest of you may derive a sense of ambition. The world can be better, and guess what: Perhaps you can help to make it better. Perhaps you can make a real difference. If you have a teacher who bucks the norms and delivers to her students far and above what the education system expects her to, you may be inspired to do the same whatever your chosen vocation turns out to be. When you finally enter the workforce, you naturally look at inadequacies in the system and ways to resolve them. It is not part of your job scope, but it has become a part of your life purpose to make your chosen work world better.

Yet... you realize that the world is not exactly waiting for you to change it. Working in a large corporation, you have been told time and again: *Stop trying to be special. Just do your job.* There are people who have given you a pat for what you are trying to do, but when push comes to shove, they backed down in favour of the status quo. You realize that yours is a lonely journey. You start to question your decisions.

Can any of us really change the world?

The Iron Cage and A Radical Escape

If this heading does not ring a bell, the exposition below may distress you. It will put you at risk of a second shattering of your view of the world. This seems to be what Sociology does best these days, for those who are willing to peel back the layers masking their eyes. What Karl Marx and Max Weber will tell you is: It is not your fault. It may not even be your bosses' fault, assuming they do not own the business. The problems you face at work are much more deep-seated than that. Do you wish to proceed?

Well, that's a trick question. You cannot proceed, because you are probably in an iron cage. If you are driven by an ambition to change your workplace and your society, you face a monstrous task. For you are not in the cage with a monster; you are already *in* the monster. This monster is the cage of rationality. In this cage, you are expected to follow the rule of standard operating procedures and hierarchies. You must carry out your duties efficiently and impersonally. It does not matter who your boss is, or who the boss of your boss is. Everyone is dispensable, just another cog in a big machine. You may accrue little victories from time to time, but for all your efforts, you and your co-workers are but birds in the same cage, unable to set free.

In this cage, you cannot *be* yourself. You are alienated from yourself, because you can only produce what your organization demands, not what you truly want. For instance, when you write for a company, you must keep to their desired brand voice. When you write for a newspaper, you must keep to journalistic conventions. This is alienating because as humans, we have the capacity to create freely. It gives meaning to our existence: We live to work, whatever work it is. But when you are paid to do work for a company, you cannot fully embrace your individuality. You do not have the power to create freely. And you have to constantly deal with all the processes which distract you from the things which excite you.

How can we escape from this predicament?

The solution, which Marx proposed, is to wrest the power away from where the power lies. In our profit-driven capitalist world of greed and exploitation, the power lies with the class of people owning or controlling the means of production: Land, labour, capital, and entrepreneurship. Your boss may deny you a pay raise, but only because the capitalist system of work makes that the guiding principle for all contract negotiations. It is not a problem of the individual who owns the organization where you work. It is a problem of the entire economy. The world of work is built on private property, where most of us—called the proletariat—are paid to work *for* the select group of people collectively called the bourgeoisie. To escape the iron cage, we must abolish private property. We can only change the world by first uprooting the capitalist system. This is the radical change we all need.

Or is it not?

When the Mirage Fades

Marx's ideas of communist revolution have influenced the world in almost unparalleled ways. Masses of people have fought on the back of his ideas. The appeal of his ideas is not entirely surprising; a name as pompous-sounding as bourgeoisie surely evokes no sympathy. Yet history has not quite evolved as he envisioned. As I write, there is only a handful of countries who claim to be communist. And these societies, rather than being the exemplars of individual freedom, are marked by its suppression. Do you want to live in a world where your search results are tampered with, where you cannot pick your leaders, or in extreme cases, where a failure at work can be punishable by death?

As compelling as Marx's vision has been, we cannot deny all the ways it can go wrong and all the ways it *has* gone wrong. The bourgeoisie may always care most about making profits on the backs of other people's labour. Taking power from them gives us the hope for something better. Yet he Is too optimistic to believe that centralizing the power in the hands of a state will bring about a transition which make things better. If anything, the regulatory power of the state typically far exceeds that contained in any single private organization. They can easily make us feel more trapped than in an iron cage.

Are you then doomed to a life of exploitation and alienation? Not necessarily. It's about time to wake up from the nightmare!

There is no doubt that Marx is a revolutionary thinker. His interpretation of capitalism is prescient and explains the structural problems underlying our working lives. He developed a utopian vision of a classless society of people who works for the common good and can thus fulfill their human potential. Yet the matter of fulfilling human potential is ultimately an individual journey. You may be constrained in many ways, but this should not stop you from finding freedom within the space you have. We can increase the space for freedom by altering systems, but no system or revolution by itself can determine how well we use this space for freedom.

If you are cynical, you may dismiss any non-revolutionary approach to change as one which betrays false consciousness. False consciousness, from a Marxist perspective, describes the inability of members of the proletariat—or non-bourgeoisie—to recognize inequality, oppression, and exploitation in a capitalist society. This happens because these patterns are so prevalent in our world that we take it as a normal and legitimate state of relations. However, opening your eyes to the depth of structural problems in the world is not incompatible with keeping your eyes open to the modest opportunities for incremental change. They are not mutually exclusive. You can change the world for the better, from inside the capitalist system.

Working Within Systems

Let's start with working from the margins of systems. The spread of technology has placed capital in the reach of non-bourgeoisie, and economies have evolved to welcome entrepreneurial spirit. It has become increasingly possible for you to not only access tools to create things you like and earn money on your own, but also to create your own tools. You can go it alone online, or you can band with like-minded peers and launch a startup. Most startups grind to a stop—sorry—but even failed ventures can enrich you. Your mistakes can also turn into lessons for the next startup which comes along with a similar conviction. Otherwise, you can join an existing startup; these are the companies who most want people with the capacity to shake things up.

In these environments, you are still participating within the capitalist system. The success of your startup depends on its ability to sustain itself financially. The success of your career as a webcomic creator depends on your ability to generate enough income to pay the bills—unless you are already financially free. There is no shame in these, because it is not the absence of money, but the absence of a preoccupation with money which allows us to produce freely. And by working at these margins, you can disrupt the established orders within the respective markets. If you are producing something of value, you are doing your part in shaping the world.

What if you are more interested in driving change from the inside of large organizations? After all, whether in business or in government, these are the power players which already hold influence over the wider society. As Weber points out, large organizations tend to have a bureaucratic nature. In these environments, you are not loitering at the margins but lodged in the heart of the monster machine. Change requires a very different attitude here. Instead of hiding in the blind spots and dishing sucker punches, you have to stare down the monster in the face and get it to do your bidding.

Can a tiny cog really turn the wheels of big machines?

Seizing Sites of Contestation

For many, the point you become an adult is when your imagination gives way to reality and your dreams wither into dust. Indeed, taking off your rose-tinted glasses takes some courage. Keeping it off is a sign of maturity, of being willing to face the world in its scorching heat. Under such conditions, you naturally keep your head down to avoid the glare. You trudge ahead, just like everyone around you. It is safer this way. But is it saner to never look up and find out where it is you are heading?

If you will just look up, you may discover that the glare does not come from Big Brother's flashlights, but the lightsabers of crusading Jedis. If you step out of your ranks, you may notice that it is not a straight march you are in. There are people marching in different directions, past the gates slashed apart by the Jedis before them. At every level in a hierarchy, there are people who strive to evolve systems and processes so that more good work can be done. And some of them do succeed, no matter how small their success.

When you take distance from your particular role in a bureaucratic organization, you may observe that power is not enclosed in the hands of those at the top. The power to make decisions is concentrated at the top, but the people at the top cannot completely disregard the voices below them. You can always contest with your charisma, a form of authority which can bypass the hierarchical logic in bureaucracies. Moreover, in a bureaucracy, any decision-making power comes virtue of the official position one occupies. Most of the time, the people above you are only there for the time being. People leave. People die. Even an iron fist will have to give way someday.

You have to keep your head up if you want to seize the opportunities which arise from time to time. Even if you cannot refashion an iron cage into a clay sculpture, you can still find ways to unpick some locks within.

Whether you prefer a clay sculpture or an iron cage, whether you like the quick sprints of startups or the marathons of large organizations, whether you can live with higher risk or lower returns, there is one lesson you must keep in mind: Be strategic. You must have a plan. Passion alone does not cut it. Marx did not merely have a dream; he wrote a manifesto explaining how the revolution can be achieved. It is encapsulated in this exhortation: *Workers of the world unite; you have nothing to lose but your chains!*

It is unfortunate that his blueprint did not match the size of his ambition. Even so, others have followed his vision and gotten things done. And in recent times, social movements have sprouted out across the world with various agendas: Civil rights, women's rights, LGBT rights, environmental protection, etc. They all involve people working collectively with a plan. You, as a worker of the world, wherever you are, in whichever organization, can certainly follow in these footsteps to change the world— little by little.

~ ~

Practicum 1: Knowing What is Worth Changing

Before you start working for any form of change, there are a few critical questions to ask yourself. First: *What do you want to change?* Change can take many forms in an organization. It can be about systems and processes. It can be about job roles and responsibilities. It can be about work relationships and cultures. Goals can be small or big; they may require just one particular change or a successive series of changes. What is most important here is knowing what you really want. If all you really want is a small change, that is the only change you are capable of driving right now. Even if you think a bigger change will be good to have, you cannot convince others unless you can first convince yourself it is a top priority.

Second: *Why is the change important?* Change is not meaningful in itself. Suppose there was a change from A to B last year. This year, you want a change from B to A. Both involve changes, but are they both positive? At first glance, it may seem that the second change is not productive. It is regressing to a previous state. However, in the case that the first change had been damaging, the second change can be acceptable as a way to restore a less negative state. Even so, there is a real opportunity. You should pause to think: Will a change to C be even better?

Third: *Why do you want the change?* This can be very tricky to probe. When you try to make a difference to the world around you, your motivation may not always be noble. Often, you possess some degree of self-interest. You may be seeking to reduce your workload. You may be trying to stand out among equals so that you are best-placed for a promotion. You may be looking to burnish your resumé so that you can impress your next job interviewers. You may be hoping to prove to yourself that you are capable, or creative, or special. It is remarkably challenging to let go of all these at once. But at the very least, you should make sure that beyond these considerations, there is a larger purpose to the change that you seek. There is a cause larger than yourself that you are fighting for. This is something which you will work for without the promise of extrinsic rewards at work.

Fourth: *Can you live with unexpected change?* Fighting a monster you are in is far from easy. Even when you fail to change the system, you will have changed the relationships you have with others. While you cannot be eaten by the monster—since you are already in it—you can be targeted like a virus. Neither open aggression or subtle quarantine is conducive to your mental health. You can also be expelled from the monster; you can be sacked from the job. That will mean a loss in income, for sure. Finding another job in the same industry may be more difficult, if your bosses have strong connections. And you, being so invested in the crusade for change, may face an identity crisis. On the other hand, you may be successful. But to change the system, you may need to change as a person as well. Not everyone can live with these repercussions. You must really believe what you want to change before you even try to drive that change.

Practicum 2: Persuading Others to Join Your Fight

Once you have clear goals which you believe in, take a dose of humility: You cannot change the world alone. You can lead any given campaign, but you need the support of others around you. An appeal to friendship and camaraderie alone will not be enough in the context of the workplace. In the capitalist system, most people work to live. They work in exchange for currency to pay for their sustenance. They are not invested in the additional work of changing the system for the greater good. They do not have to help you, especially if they cannot perceive tangible and immediate benefits to the change you seek. You have to make a case which makes sense for them personally.

You need to frame the issue. Framing involves conscious strategic efforts by groups of people to fashion shared understandings of the world that legitimate and motivate collective action. There are two elements you must satisfy to get people onboard your cause. First, they must feel aggrieved about some aspect of their lives. You have to reframe personal issues others face at work into structural problems that many face. You have to conjure the socio-logical imagination, because it gives the rationale for collective action. Second, they must believe they can solve the problem through collective action. Any action you propose has to be seen as achievable within your organiza-tion. Naturally, what's achievable will vary greatly with the size of your organization and the position in the hierarchy you are in, among other factors.

When it comes to social movements, the easiest frames to use are master frames. For example, equal rights and opportunities is a master frame. Freedom of choice is a master frame. Justice is a master frame, as is injustice. Hegemony is a master frame, as is counter-hegemony. These frames are not context-specific. For instance, in-equalities can be found in every facet of social life, not just in workplaces. They are thus inclusive and easy to mobilize people around. However, precisely because master frames are less specific, there can only be a surface unity which can be hard to translate into action which really meet the goal you wish to achieve in an organization. Moreover, anyone can invoke these frames. If opposing parties appeal to the concept of fairness, what sets one apart from the other? To make your case, you must always tie master frames back to the contextual level to rally others around your cause.

To deepen your persuasion of others, you have to be imaginative. You have to be a storyteller. You have to connect your goal and desired actions to events and experiences which others can observe or identify with. It is important to make sure that you are not spinning far-fetched tales entirely out of imagination. You have to—if not practically, then ethically—ground your narrative on real happenings. The challenge is to splice fragments together in a relatively unified and compelling manner, so that it can resonate with others. It is equally important to remember that you cannot be fully objective in the process. Even when you stick to real happenings, you will intuitively highlight the portions which best support your story. It is necessary for effective persuasion.

Practicum 3: Adapting to Changes in Situations

If you have a single aim which can be met with one specific and achievable action, your battle should be relatively easier to fight. As long as it does not compromise the positions of others in the organization—whether superiors or other teams—all you need is a convincing message and the right timing. Once your goal is achieved, your crusade is over. The movement ends. But if you are more ambitious, you will likely want to bring about several changes over time which represent incremental steps towards what you believe is best in the organizational setting. Sustaining a movement requires a more concerted effort, because you will have to take ownership of actions previously taken.

If you hope to drive a series of incremental changes, you may have to adapt the frames you use over time. The first reason is that situations change. If you succeeded in driving a specific change, the implications of the change will soon become apparent. If it is well-received by most, you will have greater bargaining power to influence subsequent changes. But if it evokes tensions in some groups, you may have to adapt your frames to account for these pain points in order to push for subsequent changes. Otherwise, your hard-fought changes may easily unravel. The second reason is that the people you work with change. Different people perceive the same thing differently. A change in boss can be all the difference between change and status quo.

There are a few discursive strategies you can use to adapt existing frames. First, you can bridge two or more ideologically congruent but structurally unconnected frames regarding a particular issue or problem. Second, you can amplify selected values or beliefs already used, particularly those which contain more swaying power. Third, you can extend beyond your primary concerns and include others which may matter more to others, in order to win their support. Fourth, you can transform old understandings and meanings of the frames and generate new ones which may resonate better at any given point in time. These strategies should not be applied haphazardly, because any shift in the narratives you present has the reverse potential of alienating some of your supporters.

It will be good to tie the narratives back to actual successes and failures of the movement thus far. For supporters, it is vital to be able to see what they have contributed to. Success can take many different forms. Have you swayed an important decision? Have you altered an organizational practice? Have you won acceptance from your bosses? Have you garnered support among external stakeholders? These can all be used as motivation to keep supporters in your fight. Conversely, it is hard to trust someone who only paints rosy pictures and pretends that failures do not exist. Do not fear failures. Failures can be used to inform future strategies. Be honest to yourself. Why has there been little support? Why has there been no change? Why has a change been ill-received? How can things be done better? If you stay focused and clear-headed, you stand a better chance of persuading others that success is not too far away.

Practicum 4: Mobilizing Networks Beyond Your Division

However, it may be useful to take another dose of reality: You cannot change the world alone. Even if you have the charisma and perceptiveness to gather coworkers around your quest, you should remember that you may one day leave the organization. If your ambition is not merely self-serving, you will be concerned about the legacy you leave behind, and whether it can sustain itself. To really sustain movements, you cannot rely on the personal charisma of any individual. You have to build a community with clear goals and tactics which can carry on the fight even after a key leader leaves.

While the previous elements can theoretically be driven by you alone, you cannot realistically expect to do everything yourself. The more people you have not just supporting you, but working alongside you, the higher the likelihood of any success. Having people working with you keeps you motivated and shields you from the burnout which may often arise as a result of being a lone agent of change. But the benefits go far beyond that. Not only can they bring different perspectives which can help refine framing strategies, they will also be willing—by virtue of being personally invested—to tap upon their own social capital and garner the support of people you will otherwise be unable to reach.

Bureaucracies typically operate in silos, with job tasks and responsibilities often divided across divisions and departments. This can yield a zero-sum game, where divisions are always vying for recognition and resources at the expense of their counterparts. Yet the goals of these divisions are not necessarily in conflict. Often, they may share certain motivations and values. The challenge is to reach across the aisles to people in other divisions and foster solidarity through the power of reframing. Building these networks of informal relations will help your goals to gain traction, potentially yielding positive actions not originally planned from your particular position in the organization. The movement can then be said to have a life of its own, with its success not dependent on the efforts of any single individual, but the collective.

This is perhaps the most you can achieve within an organization. Yet as large as an organization may be, you can always take your work outside it. Once you have invested enough effort in reaching out to different people, you may be in a position to start an association with others. The defining difference is that the site of contestation is no longer an organization, but the larger society. This brings a lot more questions to the fore. How narrow or wide should your focus be? Which issues are top priorities? Who are your friends and who are your opponents? How can you gain material resources to sustain operations? When will be a good time to mobilize resources to fight your cause? And how would success look like? These are all huge question marks hanging over all social movements.

Changing the world is hard. Changing the world for the better is even harder. People who summoned the courage to fight for change at any level, from their family and community to their society and nation, have to live with misunderstanding and condemnation. Changing the world is not for everyone. This is no shame. You can only drive change when you truly believe what you want to change. But don't let fear drown you in the status quo. Listen to the rumblings in your heart. Discover what you care about. Perhaps you will find the particular ways you can make a difference at work, however small they are. You may not ultimately change the world or even your workplace, but in bucking the norm this way, you will have found your own voice. What more can you ask for?

4

Recess: Weaving Webs of Interaction

Lend me a hand!

When I was in primary school, we had 30 minutes to recess every day. Recess is a curious term to use, because these periods typically involved peak levels of physical exertion—at least for me. The five minutes tops I spend grabbing a frozen syrup stick is but preparation for the real task at hand: *Iceman*. Iceman is, where I lived, an oft-found variation of the game of catching. The team of catchers can freeze the runners by touching them, in which case the frozen runner is not allowed to budge from the posture they had at the instant they were touched. However, a runner can unfreeze one of their own in the same way, as long as they are not in the frozen state. The game ends when all the runners are frozen, or when the bell rings!

It amazes me now how we could play the same game every day the sun is out. I suppose that being kids, sitting in the classroom builds up tensions in the body which must be relieved once we can get up from our desks. To be clear, not everyone joined. Yet not everyone who joined was sporty. There must be something in the game more than detoxification. Was it the thrill of competition? Was it the quest for social acceptance? Was it the desire for physical bonding? Was it the culture of helping, of lending a hand to a frozen runner so they get to play again?

As you grow up, these wants don't really change. Sometimes you strive to stand out from the crowd. Sometimes you try to fit in with the crowd. Sometimes you run in the park where you can see others running. Sometimes you stop running your race to help others with theirs. You will want some more than others; there should be little stopping you from pursuing what you want. Yet when it comes to the workplace, the spaces where you spend most of your adult life in, somehow the rules of the game change.

This is the story many are told: There are no friends at work. Every man for himself and every woman for herself. It's like you are still playing Iceman, except in this perverse version you don't know who is a runner and who is a catcher. You don't know whether that friendly coworker will suddenly grab your wrist and shout *Freeze!* You have no clue if there is any runner at all who can save you when you need a helping hand. In this climate of fear, it is far easier to behave like a catcher. You don't want to harm others, but at least you can stay safe in your armour. How heavy though, to keep that armour on for decades with no recess.

Can we rewrite the rules at work?

Who Are You, Really?

The rules of the social world are not cast in iron, because humans are not programmed beings. As you grow up, you will have met different people and belonged in different groups. Each of these groups will have its dynamics influenced by its members. If you look more closely at your memories, you should find that you behave differently in different groups, whether in a pair of two or in a pack of dozens. You may also notice that you behave differently with the *same* person in different group settings. Are you really one self or a collection of selves?

This is when we apply the third lens of Sociology. Unlike the big ideas of the functionalist and conflict perspectives in the previous chapters, symbolic interactionism is concerned with the interactions among individuals, the micro processes which work to form what we perceive as our everyday lives. It originated from the ideas of George Herbert Mead, though it was his student Herbert Blumer who came up with the term. The idea is that humans are meaning-making beings who interpret situations within the specific contexts in which they occur. As your social circles expand and evolve, you learn to interpret the unwritten rules in them and adapt your behaviours accordingly.

Here comes the implication: The people you hang out with shapes the person you become. And it is not as straightforward as you think. Charles Cooley captures it succinctly with this eloquent statement: *I am not what I think I am, and I am not what you think I am. I am what I think you think I am.*

This mental puzzle brooks an illustration. Suppose that *I* think I am quite a dumb person, because my life is full of questionable decisions. But this doesn't necessarily mean I am dumb. Suppose that *you* think I am a smart person, presumably because you feel enriched by this book you are reading. Again, that's just your opinion; it doesn't mean I am smart. Yet your opinion may have an influence on my opinion. If *I* believe that *your* opinion is valid, I may end up behaving in ways which reinforce that opinion. For instance, if all of you published glowing reviews which I find genuine, I may proceed to write more books. (I see what I did here.) Yet if *I* believe that *your* opinion is invalid, I will behave in ways which disprove that opinion. I may post silly videos and spew rubbish on my public social media accounts.

In both scenarios, I will have moved on from a previous state of being. I may try to live up to your expectations, or try to play it down. I may try to satisfy your tastes, or steer clear of them to hold on to my personal voice. Whatever it is, each opinion has the potential to leave an imprint on our selves, at least within the context it was voiced in. You can never truly unsee an opinion you have read or unhear an opinion you have heard about yourself. Whether consciously or unconsciously, you make sense of these opinions and decide how to respond. This shows how your identities are socially constituted. You are continually becoming what you think others think you are.

Going with the Flow

While you can ideally pick the most healthy response each time, it is not always practically possible. More often than not, you are likely to respond in a way that avoids conflict. Think back to the last time you did a group project in school. Can you remember a specific discussion you had with your group mates? Try to recall a point when there was disagreement. Perhaps it was about the choice of topic. Perhaps it was about the structure of the report. Perhaps it was about the delegation of work. When you disagreed with something a group mate said, did you voice it out in full force right away?

Chances are, you did not. You might have waited for an opening to bring up your views later on. You might have been persuaded. You might have decided to let it pass altogether and just follow what was suggested. This tendency to avoid conflict results in what Erving Goffman described as the "veneer of consensus", where each participant in a social interaction conceals their true wants in order to maintain a working consensus. You may not necessarily agree with what the group is doing and how it is being done.

But you do try to follow the social pact to avoid conflict and not encroach on the areas others see as important.

On the flip side, you might be one of those who likes to take the lead and set the terms of discussion. You will find too that it is really not that difficult. The key lies in first impressions. If you are meeting your group mates for the first time, you have a great chance to establish your authority. If none of your group mates project a similar persona, you are in the driving seat to lead all subsequent discussions. They will let you, because they can infer that it is important to you and will likely respond in ways to avoid standing in your way. But if you later step back or show yourself to be incapable in the role, another group mate may feel justified in stepping in.

What symbolic interactionism shows is that your self is always embedded in social situations. The basic rule of the social world is that you have to respond to each new bit of stimuli. However strongly you hold on to an image of yourself, you cannot go through life without being changed. This is nothing to be ashamed of. The process helps you to evolve as individuals as you grow older. Yet there is ever the risk that you may find yourself in an environment where you cannot dictate the norms, and which compels you to behave in ways you are unwilling to. Like in the workplace.

Emotional Labour at Work

In her landmark book published in the 1980s, Arlie Hochschild examined how flight attendants are expected to perform emotional labour. Among airline workers, the flight attendant has the most contact with passengers. They thus become the face of the airline, with advertisements selling the image of flight attendants with omnipresent smiles and inflating the expectations of would-be passengers. Accordingly, airlines put in place recruitment and training programs which seek to hire and groom attendants with the skills to meet these sky-high expectations.

Where Hochschild did her research, flight attendants are tasked with conveying a relaxed atmosphere just like home. Because home is safe. Home does not crash. Yet this is just a basic requirement. The metaphor of home has to go deeper into the heart if these flight attendants are to manage in-flight contingencies with poise. Passengers should be treated as children, to be cajoled when they throw tantrums. Passengers are siblings who can get jealous when you appear to treat other passengers better. Passengers are not always right, but they are never wrong. No matter what happens, flight attendants are expected to never retaliate with anger. They just have to divert their anger, whether through distraction, silent venting, or talking it out with another flight attendant, who is likewise expected to preach calm.

It can yield positive experiences for those who believe in acting deeply for the sake of delivering excellent service. Receiving cues of satisfaction and appreciation from passengers can be quite empowering, assuring flight attendants that there is meaning to their emotion work. Yet industry changes have made this increasingly untenable. As travelling becomes more prevalent, airplanes have to expand and fly more often to meet demand. For cost reasons, companies decided not to maintain the attendant-passenger ratio. This means that flight attendants have much less time to perform deep acting with each passenger, and much less time in between flights to recharge so that they can bring their service A-games. There is now no choice but to resort to surface acting. As Hochschild puts it, half-heartedness has gone public. Airlines have adapted their strategies accordingly to compete more on price and safety.

You can probably identify with the sensation of emotional labour in your own lives, especially if you have entered the workforce. Whether you work in a team of ten or thousands, you are most likely to have seen or heard about people playing office politics. These involve the use of power from position and social relations to get what you want. It is a game often associated with superficiality. Usually it manifests in destructive ways, with some abusing authority to the detriment of others. You have probably rolled your eyes or shuddered behind someone who always speaks animatedly with a pasted-on grin. Because the social world requires you to respond to every action, talking to such people can exhaust you. If deep acting does not cut it with you—assuming it's even possible—surface acting can at least maintain harmony and keep conflicts at bay.

Can we only accept acting as a fact of working life?

Weaving Webs of Interaction

It is true that you cannot completely distance from the social relations in your workplace. It is true that playing along can help you to avoid unnecessary conflict which will cause your emotional health to suffer even more. It is not true, however, that you *only* play along to the rules set in place. As long as you do not allow yourself to be swallowed up by dirty politics or the fear of it, you can always add new rules of your own. You can always play your own game.

Let's think about Iceman again. In the workplace, the catchers are those who play dirty politics for their own gain. The runners are people like you and me, who care about being good people. In a climate of fear—of exploitation and backstabbing at work—you can be forgiven for retracting to your armour and behaving like a catcher, even when you are not one. You become wary and keep others out. No friends at work, as they say. Yet this is far from ideal. When you see a runner being frozen, what will you do? If you choose to hide, and all the other runners choose to hide, the live runners will dwindle and the catchers are bound to win. But if you lend a helping hand to your fellow runner, it is game on. You cannot win, but you may not lose.

This may seem like work without rewards. If your hands are already full with the weight of your formal responsibilities, why would you want to extend them to others? Well, sometimes you just have to do the right thing. As Desmond Tutu puts it, "If you are neutral in situations of injustice, you have chosen the side of the oppressor. If an elephant has its foot on the tail of a mouse and you say that you are neutral, the mouse will not appreciate your neutrality."

The capitalist workplace tends to perpetuate a self-serving culture in which we play along to the dictates of hierarchy. This severely constrains the possibilities of finding your voice at work. Do not let it. If you take no interest in strategically driving institutional change, what you can do is to stand up for others and lend a hand to those in need. The good thing is that you can do this at any level, regardless of your position in the hierarchy. It takes effort and potentially puts you in a more vulnerable position. Yet taking this risk can come with the reward of forming genuine bonds with the runners around you. And how you choose to interact with others at work will shape the person you become, not just at work but outside it. Is this not more valuable?

Keeping the well-being of others in mind is a good start. The spirit of lending a hand to others is the best antidote to cold-hearted office politics. If you believe this can add purpose to your working life, then you should equip yourself with skills which can help you to help others more effectively. As you take a pause from formal work responsibilities, and weave webs of genuine interactions with the less empowered, a culture of warmth may just catch on. Start rewriting the rules of the game!

~ ~

Practicum 1: Noticing Who to Support

In Iceman, it is obvious who needs help. They can be all be seen frozen in their steps, while the rest of the school goes about their activities. At work, because runners complicate things by wearing armours, you will need to pay closer attention. There are two dimensions to look at: Social webs and psychological dynamics. The social webs at work can be further split into institutional roles and informal relations. You can derive from these at least three types of people who can do with a good dose of social support.

First, people who are lower in hierarchies. These typically involve the interns, the temps, the junior staff. As they occupy the positions with least authority, there is a high chance that they will be exploited. Errant bosses may be abusive in their language and push these juniors into the flames when mistakes are made. Often, these juniors may be in their first or second working stints and never exposed to such environments. This makes them highly vulnerable, especially for those who take the torrent of abuse on their shoulders into their hearts. Even when the interns and junior executives are not subject to abuse, they are often handed thankless errands and not given the space to express and develop themselves. As you move up the hierarchy, you will probably notice similar dynamics being replicated, with junior managers at the mercy of their superiors' whims.

Second, people who are isolated from social circles. While formal roles constitute the primary social web in the workplace, informal networks exert a significant influence on one's lived experience. The smaller the organization, the more this effect is magnified. Whether it is due to personality differences or misunderstandings, some people may be consistently excluded from conversations and lunches. Imagine spending 40 hours every week with people around but no one to talk to. It can be somewhat freeing to some people, but the lack of a recourse can make them clam up and unwittingly take its toll. Besides this, there are specific job roles which either keeps one at the margins or right in the middle of nowhere, without a team to belong to. People suffer physically when they lack social support, and those in such positions may find such support hard to find, especially when the interpersonal climate is not the most friendly.

Third, people who are maladjusted. This can affect anyone, regardless of their position in the hierarchy and their integration in informal social relations. Using the symbolic interactionist lens, Susan Harter identified four ways a person can have maladjusted identities. One, you can incorporate others' unfavourable opinions of you and have low self-esteem. Two, you can fail to internalize others' opinions and compulsively live for others' approval. Three, you can develop multiple social selves in response to different contexts which come into conflict with each other. Four, you can suppress your true self to meet others' expectations. While all of us are susceptible to the social world in these ways, there are some who become especially maladjusted and are unable to extricate themselves. This may actually affect those near the top most, because they risk falling further if they let go of what took them up there.

Practicum 2: Deciding Who to Support

After noticing the specific people in your workplace who might need help, you have to ask yourself truthfully: Who are you in a position to help? Following from the previous section, there are two dimensions to consider: Social webs and psychological dynamics.

First, are there social barriers hindering closer interactions? In the workplace, each position comes with its official set of responsibilities. These responsibilities are often coupled with behavioral expectations, especially the higher one climbs the organizational hierarchy. For instance, a director may be expected to maintain distance with their subordinates. It can be a deliberate move to project authority and maintain impartiality. Putting pressure on directors who typically eat alone to join the team everyday for lunches will not land you in their good books. Conversely, a new junior executive will generally be more grateful for your invitations. Similarly, you should be sensitive to dynamics existing across different teams. If two teams are at loggerheads, you may not want to reach too far into the other team, because this may not be taken kindly by those in your team.

Second, are your personalities compatible? Sometimes you can just follow your gut. There are some people you can click with from the first time you meet, and there are others who you just cannot warm up to after years of acquaintance.

Generally, the more similar your personalities, the easier it is to understand them and communicate effectively with them. Yet compatibility can vary at work. In the workplace, working styles become important as well. Since every job is different, each pair of positions will entail a different working dynamic. Sometimes a click can become a clash at work. Other times a clash can become a click at work. The people who you can support effectively are those who you can click with on some level, whether personally or in a direct working relationship. If you find it difficult to identify personality fit, you can try self-assessment tools such as RIASEC and MBTI.

It is not that you cannot reach out to people who are quite different from you in position and personality. But it is more valuable to look out for those around you first, because you may well be the best-placed person to lend a helping hand. It is also more realistic, because before you lend a hand, you should make sure you are in a good position to lift them up. The further you extend your hand, the more likely that you will lose your own footing.

Practicum 3: Lending a Helping Hand

Noticing the ones who are powerless, isolated and maladjusted should not be difficult once you pay attention. The same goes with identifying the ones you are actually in a position to help. The tricky bit is how you can help. It may help to take a pause here and consider how you view these individuals, because your opinion of them will influence how you decide to help. Read these statements and see if you agree or disagree with them: *They've got to stand up for themselves. They've got to take the initiative. They've got to sort out their own problems.*

If you agree with the statements, there is a danger that you actually blame them for their own plights. You may think of yourself as a discipline master, pointing out how they are inadequate and telling them how to behave better. I don't think you like to be reprimanded by people who always think they know best. Each individual has their own life history, with a series of environments heavily shaping who they have become. If you are unable to extend empathy for people's plights, for how difficult certain changes in mindset or behavior are for them, then perhaps the best you can do is to not intervene at all. Stepping in recklessly will most likely put them in a more defensive and misunderstood position, making it even harder for the next person to help.

If you disagree with the statements, there is a danger that you will keep them disempowered. You may think of yourself as a superhero, stepping in at every juncture to rescue them. When you turn words into actions, others will certainly be more appreciative. On the flip side, they may come to rely on you to stand up for them, to include them in conversations and lunches, to put out the fires they unwittingly set. Even if you are willing to keep up your efforts, such dependence is not sustainable. If you switch department or leave the job, or if they do, the old problems will play out again as intensely as ever. Your efforts would have largely been in vain.

Lending a helping hand to these people is not as easy as it sounds. You have to be empathetic and tactful, yet also inch them forward in working on their personal problems. There are thus two facets: To affirm, and to equip. Every person constructs stories of their own lives which inform how they behave. There is logic behind seemingly senseless behavior. If you can reach out with an open mind to listen to these stories, you will be able to understand where they are coming from. Then instead of stepping into their space and telling them they are doing things wrongly, you will naturally affirm what it is that they are doing with their lives in all its convoluted imperfections. The best kind of support one can receive is a listening ear.

It is only when you can understand another person, and make that person feel understood, that any attempt at sharing advice can be met with trust and not defensiveness. Even so, instructing people what to do is never wise at any stage of a relationship. When you recognize others as humans just trying to live their lives sanely, you will not tell them what to do. You will share things and experiences—

like books, courses, profiling tests, heart-to-heart talks—which can help them to decide what to do. Exactly what this entails, you have to figure out with an open mind and a kind heart.

Practicum 4: Extending Your Interpersonal Influence

Each person you decide to support—more than what is convenient for you—is an ongoing project. Each project requires continual effort. You must not think that you can cut off the bond once you have done what you set out to do. Every social action will elicit a response. If you suddenly recoil from someone, all the affirmation you have given will suddenly turn into rejection. They may construe it as a failing on their part and lose any confidence that you may have helped them to gain. It is thus vital to extend support in ways which are sustainable for you. You should not hurry to weave new webs of interaction if it places high risk on the relationships you are already building.

Yet when the supportive relationships have reached healthy states or yielded healthier outcomes, the maintenance required will drop. You may then feel justified in reaching out to more people, even those who you do not seem as well-placed to lend a helping hand to. For instance, people who work in competing departments, people who are levels higher in the hierarchy, and people who have quite different personalities from you. The more different and distant someone is, the less you can possibly do. You cannot move as quickly since these people will be less receptive to your overtures. Even when you manage to overcome the barriers, you have to be ready to navigate the judgments from those around you.

While this can appear quite a thankless endeavour, there can be rich rewards should you do it right. Organizations often stretch hierarchies and retreat into silos the larger they become. In such politicized environments, self-protection becomes the name of the game. No one wants to be seen as a runner, because it makes them vulnerable. It is risky. But if you have the courage to buck the norm, to play a different game, you have the potential to turn some heads in a good way. And when you reach out across the aisles, the very aisles which most divide organizations, then you are in effect trying to rewrite the rules of the game. If you can soften these boundaries, you will have done something special.

Even if you prefer to work with those close and more similar to you, and not test these boundaries, you are already doing more than what you are responsible for. You are thinking for others, not just yourself. You are lending a hand when no one truly expects you to. To take a pause from formal work responsibilities, and interact in ways which can alter the social dynamics for the better of the less empowered, is perhaps the noblest thing you can do in a capitalist world. Weaving webs of genuine interaction at work is perhaps our best hope of keeping humanity flowing through the core of our society.

5

Assess: Probing Pitfalls and Intersections

Can you do everything?

Two poles exist in Sociology. The first involves notebook scribbles and interview transcripts. The second involves survey printouts and data tables. While they take very different skills and carry very different attitudes to the quest for knowledge into the social world, they have to stop at the same final step: Distilling the data. As convinced as you are of the importance of every single sentence or digit, you cannot put everything into your thesis or your presentation. You have to cherrypick the ones which can most effectively communicate the story that you see.

I never learned this lesson as a Sociology student. Whatever mention of it must have been drowned in the torrent of readings designed to open yet another way of thinking about things. When the discipline is predisposed to challenging common sense, it could usher in a "but then" attitude. I could never settle on a point of view because there is merit in each, and even if it were possible, fusing them proved too onerous within the academic timetable. It was only in the working world that I learned about the marketing funnel and data storytelling. You have to know what you want to achieve, then angle your approach towards it.

The same goes with The Sociology Practicum. You have now journeyed with me through three empowered approaches to work, built on three schools of sociological thought. I hope you can see the value in each approach. But now is the time for you to decide what it is that you really want. As with the sociological perspectives, there are contradictions among these approaches to work. They are not always compatible, especially not within the limits of a human body. You cannot live three different lives at once. The more you complicate your mind, the more you risk coming across as phony. You will only confuse and alienate your coworkers, making any goal you have more difficult to achieve.

Although I have given them names which are easy to remember—Express, Transgress, Recess—there are pitfalls which can be tricky to navigate. Each can entail repeated cycles of three steps forward, two steps back. You have to continually respond to changes around you and inside you, to stay on the right track and stride forward purposefully. Picking one approach is already a handful. In trying to juggle multiple approaches, you risk failing to really embrace the spirit in each of them.

That said, there are compatibilities between the different approaches to work. While staying focused is important, it is counterproductive to become fixated on a particular way of doing things. Each approach involves blind spots which, when left untended, can make you give up even when you are on the right track. The solution, then, is to find and apply lessons from the other approaches without deviating from your chosen one.

~~

Pitfalls of Express: Exhaustion and Stasis

Suppose you find self-expression to be of most importance. You will take time to profile your career personality. You will identify occupations which have a close fit to your personality and seek those which can allow you to develop your skills and interests. When you face relational obstacles in a job, you will pay attention to the people working around you, to find more optimal ways of working with people who are similar to or different from you. You will continue to do this as people come and go. You will also pay attention to the specific tasks which occupy your working hours and feel for signs of resistance in yourself. You will assess whether your goals have changed, or whether your issues stem from the organization's goals and structures.

Even if you have done your homework, there is a problem which afflicts many across the private and social sectors: Lack of time. The lack of time stops you from producing your best work, even if your employer may value your gifts and encourage you to express them. If you work in a news media organization, you have to deliver an article quickly or it might quickly drop into irrelevance. If you work in a market research agency, you cannot spend an entire week stringing a fascinating story for a single client and ignore the other five or ten. If you work in a school or social service organization, you cannot give all your compassion to one person and neglect the rest. More often than not, organizations have less manpower than they need. When keeping up is a problem, consistently giving your best work or self is a tough ask.

You may try to anyway, putting in far more hours than required to go the extra mile. This is understandable when you have a strong passion for what you do. Sometimes it is precisely the work in those extra hours to delight others which gives meaning to your working life. It is all good if you do not have priorities outside work. Yet chances are, you do. In pouring your entire waking self into work, you are eroding the bonds you have with your family and friends. You are putting yourself at elevated risk of a breakdown in your physical and mental health. Life is not all about work. When your life becomes all about work, you gradually lose the capacity to function optimally. A body in protest mode will not find work very enjoyable.

Conversely, a job can also become too comfortable. When the novelty fades, you may find yourself just going through the motions. For instance, you may be a content editor for a shampoo brand. You like this brand—you use it personally—so you enjoy writing blog articles for them. And where articles wear and tear, you stylishly repair. Two years in, you still have no difficulty in coming up with new angles and evolving the company's content strategy. Your bosses are absolutely pleased with your work. Despite this, you do not find yourself to be growing. You feel as though you have hit an internal plateau. Comfort has turned into resistance.

When resistance creeps into your job, as in these scenarios, the pitfall is deciding to leave prematurely. You believe that these problems can only be resolved on job portals. You feel even that you have earned the right to leave, because you have given your all. But if there are a lot of positives at your current workplace, it may be worthwhile to exhaust your possibilities with them first.

Lessons from Transgress and Recess

An obvious solution to exhaustion is to negotiate an internal change in job position. To do so, you have to know the specific change you will need to address your difficulties. You also have to learn to speak up for yourself. This requires the kind of strategic and vocal mindset espoused in *Transgress*. If you are struggling with relentless news cycles, find out which topics can afford you more breathing space. Then explain your situation to your boss. If you can volunteer quality work which proves your ability in those arenas, you may be next in line to any vacancies which arise. It is easier to find a suitable role in your current organization than elsewhere, especially if you can see your coworkers in action from the inside.

Sometimes, it is possible to ask for flexible working arrangements. This includes working from home and shortened work hours or work weeks. While much is dependent on the organization's receptiveness, the general trend is favourable for you and me. If these options are on the table, you have to be clear what you really need. Can you work as productively outside an enclosed office? Can you live on the reduced income from a shortened work week? Which responsibilities do you have to let go so that your work-life balance can be restored? You have to make sure your proposed solution will address your pain points directly. Then, as above, you have to position your request in a way which assures your employer that the quality of your work will not be compromised.

If you are neither willing to leave your current position nor work flexibly, there is a third option: Evolving the job requirements. The boundaries of jobs are not fixed. Compare yourself to the person who occupied your exact job position five years ago. Did you do the same things? Chances are, no. That position might not even have existed then. Organizations restructure from time to time when the leaders change or when the markets change. With technology, new work activities emerge and old ones disappear. Many new activities can be, ironically, rather menial. Even if you are passionate about your work, there are likely tasks which distract you from the real work. You can turn this problem into an opportunity by advocating for changes which can truly increase efficiency and free up time for the value-added tasks. And you may suddenly find work-life balance more achievable.

If comfort is the source of your resistance, the above solutions can bring you down a new challenge with far fewer unknowns than moving to another organization. Even working fewer hours or from home can free up time for you to pick up courses and hone work-related skills within the time originally meant for work. There is another solution in the vein of the *Recess* approach: Mentoring. Whatever work you do, there is always a need for training and development.

If you are content in your job but lacking stimulation, try extending a hand to offer guidance to others, especially if you are in a more senior position. When you become a mentor, a good one at that, your perspective and style will rub on your mentees and show in traces of their work. This means you are effectively channelling your expression through others. And you too will grow from the process.

While these solutions borrow from the perspectives of the other two approaches, they do not depart from the central goal of self-expression. You remain on your quest for paths of lower resistance, as smoothly as you can.

~ ~

Pitfalls of Transgress: Inconsistency, Egoism, and Conflict

Suppose you want to drive change in your work institution. You will take time to think about what exactly you want to change and why you want to change it. You will ask if it is really worth changing and brace yourself for any potential consequences. Once you are sure of yourself, you will try to bring others into your fight, through the power of framing. You will tell stories grounded on real happenings, though stories can never be fully objective. As your movement progresses, you will find ways to adapt to new situations, whether caused by changes in personnel or changes you successfully fought for. You will strategically evolve your frames and share leadership with a few to keep the support for your movement going strong.

When you hustle for support, you may say different things to different people. When you have an idea what each person wants, you will naturally tell an inflected version of the story of your movement which satisfies those wants. This maximizes the likelihood that they will fall in your line. However, the line between constructive and destructive politics can be quite hard to discern. Things get tricky fast when you come across as a different person to different people. When these people talk to each other, they may arrive at the conclusion that you are a multi-faced person who will say anything to anyone in order to get what you want. Such distrust is deeply counterproductive, not only for you as a person but for the goals you stand for.

Faced with judgments, you run the risk of retracting into a self-serving mentality. Like with constructive and destructive politics, the line between fighting for a cause and fighting for yourself is razor-thin. You may start out genuinely fighting for a larger cause you believe in. But when others misunderstand you, you have to find a way to deal with the negative feedback. You cannot really ignore it, especially since you are actively reaching out for others' support. If you internalize it, you will question the motives of your efforts and wonder if you are actually self-serving. The movement is bound to lose steam. If you contest it, you may slip into a defensive mode and end up spending more energy fighting for yourself than the cause.

In fighting for change in the workplace, you are bound to stir up some politics. No matter how good your intentions, there will always be a fundamental conflict between change and the status quo. The status quo is always the more comfortable option. Change is not easy to deal with, let alone push for. Problems multiply when the conflict becomes personal. When factions break out within teams, the work environment becomes perpetually antagonistic. Anything you do can be used as an indictment of your character from the opposing side. When relations become this toxic, there may be no recourse but for the leaders on either side to leave. Any positive from the movement, if any, will likely be lost amidst the wounds suffered by everyone in proximity to the crossfire.

At any stage, you may choose to give up. And you may actually be wise to do so, for the sake of yourself or others around you. Unlike self-expression, the journey of transgression is greatly swayed by external factors. Timing and tact are extremely important. But instead of giving up entirely, take a break and once you are ready, think about how you can do things better next time. You may discover that your enthusiasm for change is still simmering deep within.

Lessons from Express and Recess

From a purely strategic perspective, every action should bring you to closer to your goal. It makes sense to wear as many hats as it takes to succeed. Yet unlike chess pieces, humans have minds of their own. They are not obliged to play the game you want to play. If you want to sustain the support from others, you have to be trustworthy. This entails a certain level of consistency in how you behave with different people. You also have to be sensitive to the side effects of your efforts, and mitigate them as much as possible.

To be consistent, you have to work at understanding your personality, just like those who adopt the *Express* or *Recess* attitudes. Try a type test like MBTI, which yield composite profiles rather than discrete traits. These profiles sketch a fuller portrait which can help you to set healthy boundaries for yourself, allowing you to retain a coherent self even as you tailor your approach to different people. By working on the self, you can avoid having to defend yourself only when your back is against the wall.

When conflicts arise in response to your efforts at change, as they invariably do, you ought to take a step back and consider the validity of others' complaints. Who will be affected by the change you are driving? How will they be affected? If the change compromises certain individuals or groups, especially those already in disadvantaged positions in the institution, you should find ways which can help them to adapt successfully. From their viewpoints, you are the one giving them problems. The only way you can overcome that unhappiness is to also give them solutions, and not just in a cursory way. You may have to reach out and understand their specific problems better and lend a helping hand without necessarily asking for returns. Their trust will be hard to earn, but once you do, you will have succeeded big time.

There will be times when you cannot mitigate the repercussions of your efforts at change. You then have to ask if you can live with being unpopular. Can you live with the glares and unkind words behind your back? Will this compromise your ability to keep going at work or your relationships outside work? Giving up in this case may not be a sign of weakness but an act of sanity. If you cannot stand toxic interactions, you might want to look for environments where resistance to change is likely to be less vehement. For instance, instead of large bureaucracies, join lean startups which are more likely to be receptive to new ideas. If you are still studying or contemplating a career switch, you can look up the O*Net profiles of occupations to find those with work styles which are more conducive to change—the specific kinds you are passionate about.

While these solutions borrow from the perspectives of the other two approaches, they do not depart from the central goal of change. You remain on your quest to seize sites of contestation, as tactfully as you can.

~~

Pitfalls of Recess: Burden, Powerlessness, and Poor Fit

Suppose you want to lend a helping hand to coworkers. You will look around for people who are in greater need of help, whether on a social or psychological level. You will take a look at your social position and personality and decide which are the ones who you are well-placed to help. You will remain sensitive to the ways you choose to help others, being careful to neither pin the blame on them nor do everything for them. You will reach out with sincerity to understand them. You will not instruct them what to do, but share things and experiences which can help them decide what to do. You will extend your hand to more people as you become more confident in your ability to help others.

To be in a position to help anyone, you must first open yourself to them. This puts yourself at risk of becoming too open, such that you absorb their negative energies. This is a real danger given that you want to help people who are in difficult situations. If you reach out to someone with depressive tendencies, you may have to careful not to let them seep into and take hold of your own body. If you reach out and gain the trust of a peer who is isolated from social circles, you may open a floodgate of misgivings which will colour your own attitudes towards other people.

When you direct your energies to helping people in need, you also effectively direct them away from people with greater authority. If you work in a small team with bosses who value teamwork and collaboration, you may earn unexpected brownie points. Yet this is the exception. In more bureaucratic settings, your efforts will be much less visible. You may be passed over for increments and promotions, when there are others who devote all their energies to work and overdeliver for the business. It gets tricky when you find yourself having to actively distance from authority, just so that the people you are helping can fully trust you with their inner worlds. This will paradoxically limit your capacity to help them at work.

The good thing about helping others is that you can do it anywhere, in any line of work. Whether you like or hate your job, there will be people who you can be more sympathetic towards. There will be people who can do with a helping hand, in whatever form. Yet it becomes a problem when this turns into a justification to ignore poor job fit or culture fit. When you are disconnected from the work that you do, it perpetually drains your enthusiasm at the workplace. For more introverted types, this will severely hinder your ability to reach out to others. Moreover, when you struggle to perform or fit in at your workplace, you will be in too weak a position to help anyone effectively.

If you slip into any of these pitfalls, you may decide to retract into fending for yourself. You start to withhold your concern for others, so that you can free yourself from social entanglements, deliver better work, and strive to not just keep still but move forward in your own career journey. Attending to yourself is vital, but this should never mean you stop helping others. Because helping others is a big part of what keeps you going.

Lessons from Express and Transgress

When you want to help others, it is easy to forget that it is as much about 'you' as it is about 'others'. You cannot lend a helping hand to others if you are not on a strong footing, whether emotionally, socially, or institutionally. As with the other two approaches, stepping back can help you to move further forward.

To deal with negative sentiments from those you want to help, you should maintain a healthy distance. If you are vulnerable to others' feelings, you have to cultivate the perspective of an observer. Instead of fretting along with what they shared, reflect on the why. What are the factors in the workplace contributing to those sentiments? If you adopt the *Transgress* lens for a moment, you may identify what specific change can help to address the root causes. You can then approach and seek the help of other people who are better-placed—by virtue of their position or disposition—to drive that change.

If you are concerned that taking a social orientation to work over an individual one hinders your career development, you may want to discuss with your supervisors the possibility of redesigning your job role to include more social elements. Whichever organization you work in, there is always room for mentoring and collaboration. Seen from the *Express* lens, helping others is something you like to do. Making it part of your job will allow you to express yourself more effectively, without feeling like you are constantly detracting from your responsibilities. And this will be helpful when the time comes for a review.

Nonetheless, helping others in the course of work is different from helping others on a personal level. You may be good at listening and supporting, but uncomfortable with training or leading. This is why having a good job and environment fit is important. The greater your fit for the job, the more diverse the opportunities for helping others. If you are connected to the work that you do, you are much more likely to become highly competent in it. Mentoring will naturally be seen as another way you can help others. It is thus necessary to do profiling tests like RIASEC to find supportive environments in which you can help others most effectively.

While these solutions borrow from the perspectives of the other two approaches, they do not depart from the central goal of altruism. You remain on your quest to lend a helping hand, as firmly as you can.

~~

Can You Switch Approach?

In each of the three discussions above, I have shared ways you can adapt lessons from other approaches to address some pitfalls with your chosen one. Yet even when you have to put on another lens or adopt a less intuitive strategy, you never quite deviated from your chosen approach. The borrowings are all angled towards your central goal. This is how you can always remain connected to what motivates you most, while maximizing your chances of realizing it at work. This is how you can carry a firm sense of purpose through the ups and downs of your working life.

Is this a choice you make once and for all of life? Taking the symbolic interactionist view, it certainly is not. Your identity evolves with the people you interact with and how you interact with them. As you move through life, you will be placed in new situations with new sets of expectations. All of these influence what you find most meaningful in the context of work. For instance, once you become a parent, you may no longer want to crusade for change at work, but instead find a more comfortable position from which you can express yourself independently. After a few years serving marginalized groups in the frontline, you may discover that you will achieve more by tackling larger systemic problems in a backroom policy or advocacy role. In such cases, switching approaches is certainly justified.

While you are free to switch between the approaches, you will be wise to not do so too often. This betrays a lack of deliberation over the choice. A cursory choice is not made to last. You have to take the time to look into yourself and your life history. You have to uncover the patterns in how you behave, not just at work but in everyday life. You have to find out what gives you joy. The deeper you go within yourself, the firmer your commitment will turn out to be.

This process is crucial, because making the choice is but the first step. You will face countless obstacles which make you question what you are striving to do. Being able to stay on one track, without retracting to the drawing board time and again, will allow you to focus on developing the various competencies and nurturing the relationships necessary in your quest. It is only in the repeated act of crossing these obstacles, one by one, that you go from theory to practice, and become really empowered by your chosen approach to work.

6

Finding Your Voice: To Speak and Be Heard

Follow your gut!

When I first decided on Sociology, I hardly knew what I was getting into. In those late teenage years, I could walk along malls and streets with my family, taking in nothing which distracts me from my thoughts, the thoughts I have been constantly tossing and turning in my head the past three days at home, so that I can tap furiously into the digits of my phone every abstract insight and every rephrasing of the same insight that could hold the key which unlocks my latest revelation into life.

I quickly realized I was living too much in my head. I needed to restore some balance. Just at this time, it was Open House. I headed straight to the Faculty of Arts and Social Sciences, attended sample lectures, and took home the brochures. And then I thought. If I did Psychology or Philosophy, I risked falling deeper into myself. Whereas if I did Sociology, I would be forced to think about matters existing outside me. Aha, feed two birds with one scone! I decided to major in Sociology, a good two years before I actually had my introductory module lecture. In that period, I barely read up on the discipline.

It must seem bizarre to you how anyone could make a major life decision so frivolously. But never mind the logic. I essentially followed my gut. Fortunately, this turned out to be just the right discipline for strange people like me. My first assigned reading was C Wright Mills' *The Sociological Imagination.* In it, he wrote about how personal problems are public issues, and how the solutions can only be found beyond the individual. Wow, I never thought of that! Yet somehow I could relate with it, in a convoluted way. Because at the heart of it, Sociology was my crude solution to a personal problem.

Looking back now, I think I have achieved what I set out for. I am now a much calmer person than I was. I no longer obsess over every fleeting thought as if it would change the world. I can go out with friends and listen to their stories without the intrusion of a rampant mind. The caveat is, many things have happened over the past few years which brought me closer to reality. Working life is certainly one of them. I cannot say that the years spent *studying for* Sociology classes at the expense of other activities has really helped me in this regard. After all, whatever its contents, studying is still a mental exercise.

What I can say, though, is that I have gained immeasurably from *having studied* Sociology. I have gained what I believe to be the defining purpose of education: A fresh perspective on reality. The perspective is what remains with me from four years of diligent study, after the readings have been forgotten. The reality I face now is the working world, a world which most of us have to live with for decades of our lives. *The Sociology Practicum* is precisely this: The fresh perspective I have taken into the reality of the working world.

Realistic Possibilities At Work

For the course of this book I have strived to keep your work options open, as far as they are realistic. This is an angle not commonly found within a genre of books. The reference section profiles diverse occupations and their market prospects, but rarely helps you make sense of your personal needs. The career section trains you on how to present and position yourself, but rarely pauses to listen to what you really want from life. The self-help section lights up your sense of the possible, but rarely empowers you within work contexts. There are of course books which straddle genres, but I have yet to find one which gives me the direction I need for the realities of working life.

So as they say, if there is a book you want to read, but hasn't been written yet, write it.

The book you are reading far surpasses the book I first envisioned. When I started drafting, all I had were tentative book and chapter titles and the names of thinkers and concepts which I will draw upon. I could barely remember many of their arguments, let alone know how they will fit in with mine. Yet if I only started after I have figured everything out, I will never have started. And I may have figured nothing. I trusted my instinct that I had enough to work with. I dug out old readings and notes when I had to. I reworked and removed passages when I had to. And I wrote a book I would buy if *you* had written it.

This is a book of hope: That whoever you are, whatever you do, and wherever you work, you can breathe greater purpose into your working life. I have advocated three distinct approaches to work to help you find paths to freedom within constraint. The narrative of work has predominantly been one of necessity and dread, at least for my generation. But the problem is not work in itself. We live to work, to speak through the work we produce. Only when you step back from your resistance to work can you start to make the right career decisions for yourself. Through this book, I hope to both lessen your resistance to work and increase your sense of empowerment, in work and in life.

Beneath the idealism, there is an undercurrent of realism permeating these pages. This is to the credit of the giants of sociological thought, on whose shoulders I have stood upon. In *Express*, I exhorted you to learn to live with resistance. In *Transgress*, I reminded you to be modest in your ambitions. In *Recess*, I explained to you the complexities involved in helping others. In *Assess*, I proposed that you pick and focus your efforts around a single approach in any time period. I do so because I am aware of the difficulties that anyone will face. You cannot expect to do everything you want. You have to make the most out of what you have and what you are able to do in any given work environment. Let go of the mirage of absolute freedom and you can begin the work of increasing relative freedom.

And Yet... A Unified Approach?

As I was drafting the *Assess* chapter, I took time to reflect on my own work-life situation. I have spent a year in market research. This is the working world I'm inhabiting; the reality I am facing. It is in the backdrop of a corporate environment that I have arrived at my current conclusions. But what if I were working for a cause I believe in? Would I stick by my position to focus on one approach at any time?

My gut tells me that it may no longer matter. If you perceive your work to be deeply meaningful in itself, there is no *need* to keep yourself empowered through any of the approaches. You are continually empowered by your quest for social impact. This does not mean that you have wasted your time reading this book. Even if you perceive no lack of meaning in your work, you can still find ways to amplify your voice, whether through playing to your gifts, driving institutional changes, or helping others in the workplace. It is just less important to organize around and develop continually within a single approach, because your sense of possibility will not hinge on your success in that approach.

This appears an enviable position to be in, though it often coincides with practical challenges. The capitalist economy is not designed to reward organizations geared towards social impact rather than business profit. More often than not, a socially meaningful job pays less and demands more hours. It is a trade-off which should not exist in an ideal world, but is nonetheless one we have to live with for the time being.

Is it a worthy trade-off? You will have to enter that situation and figure that reality out for yourself. Only you will know if a particular job is right for you, in your particular life situation.

Sociology's 3rd Gift: Giving Voice to the Voiceless

I opened this book by sharing two lessons I have taken from Sociology. The first is releasing the illusion of free will. The second is finding paths to freedom. For the rest of the book, I placed you at the centre of the practicum. Even when I embarked on the voyages of macro thinkers, I swiftly returned with paddles to help you swim on in the working world. This is not how Sociology is taught. This is not how

Sociology is practised in academia. But this is what I believe Sociology can be. This book channels Sociology's third gift: Giving voice.

In bringing attention to constraints, Sociology effectively stands up for people who are most constrained. These are typically those who live on the margins of society, unable to speak up for themselves. As brought up in the *Recess* chapter, the people with the least voice at work include those lower in hierarchies and those isolated from social circles. These are real people who can do with a little help, right now, where they are.

Sociologists and other social thinkers can become too hung up over what it is that can truly change society, and direct energies to downplay or even dismiss approaches other than their own. Yet theory is not reality. In reality, every action which emanates humanity has the potential to plant a seed of doubt in the status quo. You can see this happening between individuals, if you would just observe. Whether they translate into any form of systemic change is down to multiple factors beyond our individual controls. This is true whichever school of thought you subscribe to; citing Marx and Weber does not lessen the alienation employees face at work. It does not make you a more effective agent of change.

Instead of fixating on massive structural solutions, Sociology can help by fostering a spirit of giving voice to the voiceless. This means to not just speak up for them, but to persuade others to speak up for them, and to help them speak up for themselves. I hope you have found in this book the impetus to speak up not just for yourself, but for others as well. Speak for a man and you defend him for a day; teach a man to speak and you defend him for a lifetime. The same goes with women.

This will require a form of creativity which exceeds the bounds of academia. Yet if there is one discipline designed to transgress established boundaries in real life, it is Sociology. In writing this book, I am also speaking up for the discipline of Sociology. It is an oft-misunderstood and much-maligned discipline among outsiders, but it really should not be. Sociology will not secure you the most prestigious and high-paying jobs. But it strikes at the heart of our day-to-day and equips you with fresh perspective to navigate diverse facets of life more effectively. Working life is just one of them. If you too have been touched by Sociology in some way, share its gifts. Let the imagination be heard!

The Courage to Speak from Your Heart

Ultimately, Sociology is about doing good with the freedom you have found for yourself. You can take yourself as starting point, and end up displaying passion which can inspire others. You can take society as starting point, and end up catalyzing change which can benefit others. You can take the people around you as starting point, and end up radiating warmth which can empower others. There is much freedom to be found within the constraints of your workplace.

Nonetheless, it's worth remembering that as important as work is—either practically or spiritually—it is not the equivalent of life. Work is a big part of life, but work is not life. As you commit more of yourself to work, you must not lose sight of what it would mean for your life. What will you have to sacrifice in other parts of your life? Can you live with that sacrifice? If so, for how long? How about your important others? You have to keep in close touch with what really drives you on a personal level. What do you really want from life?

Given how work dominates our discussions of life, you should find work which fits in with your deepest life goals. You should find work that can help you develop into a better person, whatever that means for you. This is regardless of your choice of approach to work, whether it is to express your voice, to transgress the norms, or to recess from individualism. If you have to work hard for it, it had better be something you find meaning in working for. Then even when you fail in some way or another, you can have no regrets because in the process of working, you would have grown as a person. This is how you find your own voice, in work and in life.

Speak from your heart, and you will always be heard.

Closing Credits

I am not a sociologist, just a Bachelor's graduate. My exposure to social theorists is relatively limited. This should not matter, because *The Sociology Practicum* is not written for academic purposes. It is written for anyone who wants to find their voice in the working world. It is tailor-made for Sociology students and graduates who wish to bring along the spirit of their discipline into their working worlds of choice. Anyone expecting an exhaustive review of social theory should locate their nearest professor instead.

Nonetheless, citations are important. Citations can point you in the direction of further knowledge. They can also help you to verify that I had indeed done my readings. To make it more readable, I am not following the citation formats designed for academics. I will simply provide the author names, book or article names, and the publication years. The year is tricky to determine for more dated works because there exist many versions across different languages. And I cannot email the authors to check.

Putting Sociology Into Practice/Finding Your Voice

C Wright Mills – The Sociological Imagination, Ch 1 The Promise (1959)

Express

Émile Durkheim – The Division of Labor in Society (1984) [first published in 1893]

Émile Durkheim – Suicide: A Study in Sociology (1987) [first published in 1897]

Stjepan Meštrović – Emile Durkheim and the Reformation of Sociology (1993)

Jonathan Turner, Leonard Beeghley, and Charles Powers – The Emergence of Sociological Theory, Ch 13 The Sociology of Emile Durkheim (2011)

O*Net Online – https://www.onetonline.org/

Arnold Spokane, Erik Luchetta, and Matthew Richwine – Holland's Theory of Personalities in Work Environments (2002)

Margaret Nauta – The Development, Evolution, and Status of Holland's Theory of Vocational Personalities: Reflections and Future Directions for Counseling Psychology (2010)

Transgress

Karl Marx – Economic and Philosophic Manuscripts of 1844 (1970) [first published in 1844]

Karl Marx – Manifesto of the Communist Party (2011) [first published in 1848]

Jonathan Turner, Leonard Beeghley, and Charles Powers – The Emergence of Sociological Theory, Ch 7 The Sociology of Karl Marx (2011)

Max Weber – Classical Sociological Theory, Ch 2.3 Bureaucracy and Ch 2.6 Legitimacy and Authority, edited by Ian McIntosh (1997)

Robert Benford – Master Frame (2013)

Robert Benford and David Snow – Framing Processes and Social Movements: An Overview and Assessment (2000)

Doug McAdam, John McCarthy, and Mayer Zald – Handbook of Sociology, Ch 21 Social Movements (1988)

Doug McAdam, John McCarthy, and Mayer Zald – Introduction: Opportunities, Mobilizing Structures, and Framing Processes - Toward a Synthetic, Comparative Perspective on Social Movements (1996)

Recess

Erving Goffman – The Presentation of Self in Everyday Life (1959)

Herbert Blumer – Symbolic Interactionism: Perspective and Method, Ch 3 Society as Symbolic Interactionism (1986)

Arlie Russell Hochschild – The Managed Heart: Commercialization of Human Feeling, Ch 6 Feeling Management: From Private to Commercial Uses (2012) [first published in 1983]

Susan Harter – Symbolic Interactionism Revisited: Potential Liabilities for the Self Constructed in the Crucible of Interpersonal Relationships (1999)

The additional readings below include other works from the 3 classical thinkers, as well as further readings which have evolved my personal understanding of the discipline. Several of these I have encountered only in passing over the course of my undergraduate education. I am including them because they can serve as primers for those of you who are keen on developing your own fresh perspective on reality. If my Sociology comrades have other readings to recommend, feel free to share the joy in your reviews.

Classical Thinkers

Karl Marx – Capital [first published in 1867]

Karl Marx and Friedrich Engels – The German Ideology [first published in 1845]

Emile Durkheim – Moral Education (2012)

Emile Durkheim – The Elementary Forms of the Religious Life [first published in 1912]

Max Weber – Economy and Society: A Outline of Interpretive Sociology, Chapter 1 Basic Sociological Terms (1978)

Max Weber - The Protestant Ethic and the Spirit of Capitalism [first published in 1905]

Max Weber - The Essential Weber: A Reader, Ch 20 The Vocation of Science (2004)

Sociology as a Discipline

C Wright Mills – The Sociological Imagination, Appendix: On Intellectual Craftsmanship (1959)

Peter Berger and Thomas Luckmann – The Social Construction of Reality (1991)

Arthur Stinchcombe – Should Sociologists Forget Their Mothers and Fathers (1982)

Arthur Stinchcombe – The Origins of Sociology as a Discipline (1984)

Mayer Zald – Sociology as a Discipline: Quasi-science and Quasi-humanities (1991)

Michel Foucault – The Foucault Reader, Chapter 1 What Is Enlightenment? (1984)

I may not write another book which leans as heavily on Sociology theories. But I do expect the sociological imagination to keep shining through even when I don't make it explicit. If you like my writing style, if you appreciate my way of seeing things, if you believe that my voice can help to enrich yours, follow me on https://socioempath.com or social media and I shall see you again next time.

You have nothing to lose but your chains. You have everything to gain when it rains.

Afterword

I started to dream about writing books about 10 years ago. It has taken a while, but I am glad I waited each one of those years before writing this. I could not have written this without the four years of diligent study in university. Neither could I have done without the past year and a half staring in the face of working life realities. Beyond the obvious, there are people whose presence has allowed me to become the writer I am today, for which I must express my gratitude, in no order of merit:

I thank my English teacher Mr Jared Quek for inadvertently starting my love affair with writing at the age of 13. My high school had a system where 10-15% of our scores came from doing things beyond the curriculum. Against the grain, he accepted blogging as one such thing. From then on, there was no return. His intellect and curious conduct remain fresh in my mind. And, as if it were planned, he was also the first to introduce the word 'bourgeois' to our impressionable minds.

I thank my Sociology teachers from the National University of Singapore who have enthralled me with their sociological imagination and charisma. Specifically, I am grateful for the opportunity to learn from Dr Ivan Kwek, A/P Paulin Straughan, Prof Chua Beng Huat, Dr Vineeta Sinha, and Mr Quek Ri An. I am a quiet student by any measure, so you may not even remember me. And anyhow, we are Durkheim of people who can't get full Marx, Weber we like it or not. But I hope I have done some justice to our discipline.

I thank the ones who have, through one way or another, given me the confidence and freedom to express myself: Mrs Wong, for making me feel special at age 12 and thus cushioning what turned out to be a tricky primary-secondary school transition. My high school and junior college friends, for condoning my adolescent self-indulgence. My more recent friends, whether students or sceptics of Sociology, for showing quiet or active affirmation—or could this just be my imagination? My family, for not peeping at my screen or intruding during my periods of inspiration.

There are two friends in particular I am grateful for: Benny, whose unassuming companionship has been an immeasurable source of strength for the past 5 years. Thanks bro, for tolerating my antics! And Cheryl, a dreamer in her own right who dished up a vital insight for my final chapter. I give you a tick!

Before I close the chapter on this book, there is just one last person I wish to mention. His name is Aloysius Pang.

~ ~ ~

On the 23ʳᵈ of January in 2019 (SGT time), following an unfortunate accident during reservist training, Aloysius left this world. He was only 28. I didn't know him personally; I had never met him in person. I had seen him onscreen though, in local television dramas. He was a very promising actor and, as his flow of eulogies showed, also a remarkably decent young man well-liked by the people around him. This was a boy who took the initiative and his own money to buy drinks and sunscreen for production crew members and industry seniors. This boy then made his onscreen mother and father cry like they have lost their own son.

For me, he has been one of the very few reflections I have found in this world. It helps that we share a fair bit of resemblance in our appearance, but the affinity runs deeper. The qualities I value in myself—humility, sincerity, curiosity, inventiveness, passion for our craft—I can see in him as well. There is just one notable difference: Even when starting a business with his brother or filming in another country, he made time to create, whether picking up musical instruments or writing scripts and lyrics. He never stopped producing in the face of obligations. I did.

When I heard his condition had worsened, I prayed and prayed. When the dreaded news dropped late at night, my tears rolled. I could not sleep. I spent the next few hours writing a tribute to him in Mandarin, the language in which I have come to know him, to try to make sense of the senseless. I wrote: *I cannot make up for any of his regrets. But I can bring forth his spirit. I will stop restraining myself. I will summon the courage to work hard in pursuit of my own dreams, in the hope that I can also bring unusual meaning to others' lives. As he has.*

Since that day, my attitude towards life has started shifting. I realized it is time to start making full use of the time I have to do what I love, to create what I really want to create. I am making progress. But it is a very slow process of change, because habits of thinking formed over the years take time to untangle. I still have much work to do. I am thus releasing a token print edition of this book to mark the 23rd of January, as a reminder to keep moving in the right direction, to keep evolving as a writer and as a person.

Thank you Aloysius for coming into my life. You remain in our hearts.

In memory of Aloysius Pang